Night Errant

Translated by
Michael Pilch

from Georges Feydeau's
Feu la Mère de Madame

Samuel French – London
New York – Sydney – Toronto – Hollywood

© 1990 BY MICHAEL PILCH

1. *This play is fully protected under the Copyright Laws of the British Commonwealth of Nations, the United States of America and all countries of the Berne and Universal Copyright Conventions.*

2. *All rights, including Stage, Motion Picture, Radio, Television, Public Reading, and Translation into Foreign Languages, are strictly reserved.*

3. **No part of this publication may lawfully be reproduced in ANY form or by any means—photocopying, typescript, recording (including video-recording), manuscript, electronic, mechanical, or otherwise—or be transmitted or stored in a retrieval system, without prior permission.**

4. Rights of Performance by Amateurs are controlled by SAMUEL FRENCH LTD, 52 FITZROY STREET, LONDON W1P 6JR, and they, or their authorized agents, issue licences to amateurs on payment of a fee. **It is an infringement of the Copyright to give any performance or public reading of the play before the fee has been paid and the licence issued.**

5. Licences are issued subject to the understanding that it shall be made clear in all advertising matter that the audience will witness an amateur performance; that the names of the authors of the plays shall be included on all announcements and on all programmes; and that the integrity of the author's work will be preserved.

The Royalty Fee indicated below is subject to contract and subject to variation at the sole discretion of Samuel French Ltd.

> Basic fee for each and every
> performance by amateurs   Code E
> in the British Isles

In Theatres or Halls seating Six Hundred or more the fee will be subject to negotiation.

In Territories Overseas the fee quoted above may not apply. A fee will be quoted on application to our local authorized agent, or if there is no such agent, on application to Samuel French Ltd, London.

ISBN 0 573 12173 7

CHARACTERS

Yvonne, an attractive woman in her late twenties
Lucien, her husband, a few years older
Annette, their maid, a country girl
Joseph, a man-servant

The action of the play takes place in the bedroom of Yvonne's and Lucien's flat in Paris

Time—about 1910

NIGHT ERRANT

Yvonne's bedroom, Paris. About 1910

A modest room, but comfortable and elegant. The style of furnishing suggests luxury without ostentation; the room is pretty but not precious. On the walls hang framed modern prints, Japanese fans, etc. At the back a door gives on to the entrance hall of the apartment. R *of it is a doorway from which the door has been removed, converting it to an open archway, beyond which is the bathroom.* L *of the hall door a lady's writing-desk stands open against the wall;* R *of the desk is a chair.* UL *is an alcove with a door that leads to Lucien's bedroom;* DS *of this is the fireplace, which is surmounted by a mirror.* DS *of this, with its back slightly to the audience, stands an armchair. Thrown carelessly over the back of this armchair are a lady's vest and petticoat. A bed, with its head against the wall is* R. *At the foot of the bed there is a bench-type seat the full width of the bed. At the head of the bed,* DS *of it, there is a small table with shelves; on the table there is a nightlight, which is lit, and a medicine bottle. Also at the head of the bed,* US *of it, there is an armchair. A woman's robe has been thrown over the foot of the bed. Yvonne's slippers are* DS, *and Lucien's slippers are* US, *of the bed. The writing-desk contains writing materials and several letter-cards. On the mantelpiece there are candlesticks and a clock* C; *a carafe of water with glasses on a tray* R; *tea-making apparatus and a box of matches* L. *From the ceiling an electric chandelier is hanging, operated by a switch* R *of the door into the hall*

As the CURTAIN *rises, the scene is in darkness, lit only by the nightlight on the small table by the bed. Yvonne, in the bed, is sleeping deeply; her light and regular breathing can be heard. About five seconds after the curtain rises, a bell rings. Yvonne, not woken by the sound but nevertheless slightly troubled in her sleep, utters a long sigh and turns over under the bedclothes. About ten seconds after the first ring the bell sounds again. Yvonne opens her sleepy eyes almost as soon as the second ring is heard. She raises her head a little*

Yvonne Who is it?

There is another ring on the bell

I expect Lucien has forgotten his key. (*She throws back the bedclothes*) You're a beast to wake me up like this.

Yvonne gets out of bed; she is in her nightdress, legs and feet bare. Two more rings on the bell are heard. Yvonne is furious

All right, I'm coming!

She snatches up her robe with a cross gesture and puts on her slippers. Having no time to put on her robe properly, she drapes it round her neck like a scarf

She exits to the hall and, out of sight of the audience, arrives at the front door, which opens on to the landing

(*Off; in a surly voice*) Who's there?
Lucien (*off; like a naughty child who expects to be scolded*) It's me! I have forgotten my key!
Yvonne (*off*) I might have known!

There are sounds of unlocking as she opens the front door

(*Off*) How inconsiderate of you.

Lucien can be heard shutting and re-locking the front door

Yvonne enters. She moves DR, *climbs on to the bed and kneels on it with her back to the audience*

Go on then! Come in!

On the command "Come in", Lucien appears. He is in full fancy dress, attired as Louis XIV, under a waterproof buttoned round the neck but reaching only to his hips. Around the raised collar of the waterproof there is a knotted scarf. The whole of the back of the waterproof is blotched with water. He has white gloves that are sodden and sticking to his hands; his shoes are muddy and his stockings likewise up to the calves. On his entrance, his hands are entangled with his Louis XIV cane, an umbrella dripping with rain and a lighted candle in a candlestick

(*From the bed*) Well? It's past midnight!
Lucien (*turning on the centre light*) So it is! I'm sorry!
Yvonne (*in a bad temper*) Never mind about being sorry! Why couldn't you remember your key? It's a fine thing to be woken with a start when you're fast asleep.
Lucien (*confused*) I woke you up?
Yvonne (*in a biting tone*) Obviously you woke me up! You don't think I make a habit of staying up till this hour?
Lucien (*sincerely; as if relieved, moving over to the mantelpiece to put his candlestick on it*) Oh, well, that's all right then! (*He is just about to blow out his candle, but stops at the sound of Yvonne's voice*)
Yvonne What do you mean, "That's all right then!"? You're pleased you woke me up!
Lucien No, no! I meant that's good . . . that you didn't wait up for me.

Lucien blows out the candle, places his cane in the corner of the fireplace, and then, with his dripping umbrella under his arm, he moves towards the bed, rubbing his cold hands together under the sodden gloves

Yvonne I ask you, what sort of time is this to come home!
Lucien (*peeling off his gloves*) I couldn't find a cab anywhere! And such weather! There were no buses for Vaugirard or the Chateau d'Eau! There wasn't anything at all coming this way.
Yvonne I bet there were some earlier!
Lucien (*without conviction*) Oh, no! Hardly any . . .

At this moment, the clock on the mantelpiece starts to strike

Yvonne (*interrupting him*) Listen!

They both listen, Lucien with an expression of foreboding. As soon as the fourth stroke sounds, Yvonne makes a face

Ten past four!
Lucien How do you mean—ten past?

Yvonne (*cuttingly*) Obviously, the clock is ten minutes slow.
Lucien Perhaps it's broken . . . Just now, when I was passing the front of the station at Saint-Lazare . . .
Yvonne Yes, yes! You're going to tell me it struck midnight!
Lucien Midnight, no, but . . .
Yvonne But this, but that! It's a well-known fact: when husbands stay out all night, their wives' clocks are always breaking . . .
Lucien How you exaggerate! (*He moves to the bed*) I'm not staying out all night; here I am! (*He sits on the end of the bed*) After all, you knew I would be late back, as I was going to the Four Arts Ball! I couldn't leave before they drew the raffle . . .
Yvonne (*brooking no response*) You would have done better not to go at all! What were you doing there? I don't know what they must have thought of you, you a married man, at the Four Arts!

Lucien is still clutching his umbrella and absent-mindedly tracing patterns with it on the carpet, as one does with a stick in the sand

Lucien Oh, I promise you, they took no notice of me!

Yvonne pushes Lucien abruptly off the bed with a knee in the backside

Yvonne Look out!
Lucien (*jumping off the bed at this blow*) What?
Yvonne Your umbrella! You're drenching my carpet.
Lucien Who? Me? (*Instinctively, he bows his head to inspect the damage and a trickle of water falls from the brim of his hat*
Yvonne (*more loudly*) And your hat! That's dripping too.

Lucien, bewildered, hurries to the door to deposit his hat and umbrella in the hall

Lucien (*as he goes*) Oh! . . . I'm sorry.

  Lucien exits to the hall

Yvonne Not even to notice what you were doing.
Lucien (*off*) It's supposed to be lucky!
Yvonne (*furiously*) Oh, yes! Make a joke of it!

Lucien reappears and stands between the door and the desk. He makes a pitiful figure, as he tugs foolishly at one end of the scarf to loosen it from the collar of his waterproof

Yvonne looks at him

What a sight you are!
Lucien It's the rain!
Yvonne What a specimen! Look at those stockings! Where did you get them?
Lucien (*piteously*) From White's!
Yvonne Well! You should send them back! (*Relenting*) Ah well, why don't you take off your coat! You're not reckoning to go to bed in it, are you?
Lucien (*conciliatory*) Of course not.

Lucien takes off his coat and exits to place it in the hall

Lucien returns. Drawing his sword with a grand gesture, he goes over to the fireplace and stands it against the chimney-breast

Yvonne That's better!

Lucien returns to midstage and shivers

(*In a tone of concern*) What's the matter?
Lucien (*with a gesture to indicate that it is nothing, then*) I'm cold!
Yvonne (*mocking*) Ah! you're cold! Perhaps you expect me to feel sorry for you?
Lucien (*with an impatient movement*) No! You asked me; so I told you.
Yvonne Well! that will teach you to go out on the razzle!

Lucien draws near the fireplace and presents his hands and, alternately, each of his feet, to the hearth

(*In a pitying tone*) What are you doing there?
Lucien (*as before*) I'm trying to get warm.
Yvonne But there's no fire!
Lucien (*repeating mechanically*) There's no—what! (*He looks at the empty grate*) Oh, yes! Habit, you know. When there's a fire, that's where you put your . . . so, subconsciously . . .

Yvonne Ssse!

Lucien (*wretchedly*) It's not very kind of you to deprive me of my illusions! I was starting to feel warmer already.

Yvonne So you warm yourself with illusions, do you? Well, from now on, my darling . . . the next time you want warming up!

Lucien (*irritated, shrugging his shoulders and moving upstage*) Oh, really!

Yvonne (*returning to the attack*) No! But to think we've only been married two years and already you're leaving me at home to go off to your Four Arts Ball!

Lucien (*wildly*) Oh, please! I'm tired, you can make a scene tomorrow.

Yvonne Oh, I'm not going to make a scene, I promise you.

Lucien (*returning a little way* DS) You don't understand. If a man is not to get into a rut, he needs to get out now and again, to see a bit of life, to have experiences, to form his mind!

Yvonne (*disdainfully*) Oh, no! You listen to me! You're a cashier at the Galeries Lafayette; how is it going to help you get on in that job, to go to the Four Arts Ball?

Lucien (*piqued*) I'm not just a cashier! I'm a painter.

Yvonne (*shrugging her shoulders*) You a painter! You dabble!

Lucien (*vexed*) I dabble!

Yvonne Certainly! You don't sell your paintings, so you dabble. Do you sell them?

Lucien You know I don't sell them! Obviously, I don't. I don't sell them . . . because . . . because nobody buys them . . . otherwise . . .

Yvonne There's only one thing you have ever managed to paint well!

Lucien (*gratified by this concession*) Ah! and what's that?

Yvonne My bath . . . with enamel!

Lucien (*vexed, reaching the fireplace*) Oh, very funny! You don't understand! (*He returns to the bed*) All the same, I am more of an artist than you think! And, as an artist, it is quite natural that I should seek artistic experiences.

Yvonne (*shrugging her shoulders*) Go on! I know what sort of experiences you're looking for, so don't talk to me about art.

Lucien (*refusing to discuss it*) Oh, you always run me down, of course. (*He goes to the mirror over the mantelpiece, to retie his jabot*)

Yvonne (*straightening the bedspread*) No, but . . .

Yvonne jumps off the bed, in bare feet, runs across to Lucien and turns him round to face her

No, but tell me, if you think I'm not being fair to you, give me one example of your artistic experiences.

Lucien Oh, really!

Yvonne (*cutting*) That's no answer! Quote me one! (*She returns* DS)

Lucien (*following her*) There are so many! Wait! For instance, when the Amphitrite appears. (*He looks Yvonne up and down, with a supercilious smile*) Only perhaps you don't know what the Amphitrite is?

Yvonne Oh, don't I? As if I don't know what it is! It's a disease of the stomach!

Lucien (*flabbergasted*) What!

Yvonne Certainly!

Lucien (*sniggering*) A disease of the stomach! Amphitrite is the Goddess of the Sea!

Yvonne (*taken aback*) Ah! (*Crossly*) Oh, I know what I was thinking of! I was confusing it with enteritis!

Lucien That's nothing like it!

Yvonne Well! Anyone can make a mistake.

Lucien Well, when her procession makes its entrance, that is an artistic experience! A beautiful model, completely naked, in a shell of mother-of-pearl, attended by nymphs and mermaids!

Yvonne (*stiffly*) A naked woman!

Lucien Completely nude.

Yvonne It's scandalous!

Lucien (*complacently*) That's where you're wrong! There is nothing in the least improper about it.

Yvonne (*moving away and climbing into bed*) Really? Well, perhaps you'd like me to go round like that . . .

Lucien (*raising his arms*) Oh, well, of course, you! That's different!

Yvonne (*sitting up in bed*) So it's improper for me, but not for her?

Lucien It's not improper for models! And that one: such a figure! her breasts . . . I've never seen the like! (*He moves to the fireplace*)

Yvonne (*bowing her head, then stiffly*) Thank you very much.
Lucien (*turning, taken aback*) What?
Yvonne You're very polite!
Lucien (*raising his eyes to heaven, then*) Oh, very well! I suppose you're going to take offence. I didn't mean you! Obviously yours are very nice! but after all . . . they're not like the breasts of a model. (*He returns to the fireplace to take off his jabot*)
Yvonne Oh! Really? (*She throws back the bedclothes and jumps off the bed to charge over to Lucien, simultaneously untying the ribbons of her nightdress*) And . . . and . . . (*she reaches Lucien and turns him to face her*) and what is wrong with them, then? What is wrong with them? (*With her back to the audience, she plants herself in front of Lucien with the front of her nightdress wide open, held apart with both hands*)
Lucien (*staggered by this unexpected manoeuvre*) What? How do I know? Oh, well, perhaps, for instance, there . . . (*He is about to place one finger on the top of her bosom*)
Yvonne (*slapping his hand and stepping back*) That's enough! Don't touch me! Go and touch hers, if you want to, as they're better than mine!
Lucien Don't be silly!
Yvonne (*returning to the attack*) Go on, then, go on! Tell me what's wrong with them?
Lucien (*trapped against the* US *doorpost of the door* L, *with Yvonne literally pressed against him*) Oh, very little! Underneath, they're fine! There, you see, I'm being perfectly fair. But on top, they're a bit droopy; there . . .
Yvonne (*indignantly*) Droopy!
Lucien (*sketching an outline in the air*) They look a bit like a coat-hanger.
Yvonne (*quickly retying the ribbons of her nightdress*) A coat-hanger! A coat-hanger! Oh, it's too much! (*She catches hold of Lucien by the left arm and sends him spinning to* C)
Lucien (*not understanding what has happened to him*) Now what?

Yvonne immediately opens the door, thus uncovered, and calls

Yvonne Annette! Annette!
Annette (*off; sleepily*) Hooon?

Night Errant

Yvonne Annette, get up!
Lucien (*astonished*) Annette?
Yvonne You heard what I said!

Annette is a country girl and is suffering from a bad head cold

Annette (*off*) Badarb?
Yvonne Get up at once!
Annette (*off*) Yes, Badarb.
Lucien Why Annette? Is Annette in my room?
Yvonne (*crossing in front of him to sit on the bench by the bed*) Ah, yes, Annette! What about her?
Lucien It's a bit steep, that! Letting the maid sleep in my bed!
Yvonne Did you expect me to stay in the apartment all alone, while you were living it up? No, thank you! (*She leans on the brass rail at the end of the bed*) I was frightened.
Lucien That's the last straw! The maid in my bed! Where am I supposed to sleep then?
Yvonne Well! There, of course! (*She indicates the room* L)
Lucien With the maid?
Yvonne The maid! With the maid! No! Now that you have come home, Annette can go upstairs to her room and you can have your bed back.
Lucien What! Sleep in her sheets!
Yvonne But they're not her sheets, they're yours.
Lucien But she has slept in them, that's enough!
Yvonne (*getting up and climbing back into bed*) Oh, naturally! If it was a matter of sharing your sheets with a naked model, you wouldn't find it so distasteful . . .
Lucien (*titillated, despite himself, by this thought*) Oh, well!

Yvonne, on her knees on the bed, has been occupied with plumping up her pillows

Yvonne (*turning back towards Lucien*) There, you see! That's what I mean! (*She crawls on her knees to the middle of the bed*) You'd like that, wouldn't you? (*She reaches the end of the bed in the same way*) You'd prefer that! Pig! (*She lies down again*)
Lucien (*exasperated*) Oh! Damn it! (*He moves to the fireplace*)

Annette enters L. *She is wearing a cotton nightdress gathered at the waist and at the back, with a low neckline and short sleeves. On top of it, a woollen dressing-gown that falls below the hemline of the nightdress. She is bare-legged in felt slippers. Her hair is dishevelled, with a headband at the front and two pigtails sticking out at the back. She is still more than half asleep, her eyes drowsy)*

Annette Is it Badarb who wods be?
Yvonne (*jumping out of bed on her appearance and running across to her*) Yes, come in! You didn't hear what my husband has just said to me?
Annette (*yawning*) Dough, Badarb.

Yvonne brings Annette further into the room, so that Annette is between her and Lucien

Yvonne He said I had breasts like a coat-hanger.
Annette (*half asleep and indifferently*) Oh, did he, Badarb?
Lucien (*ironically*) Did you make the maid get out of bed just to tell her that?
Yvonne Certainly! I want her to tell you in her own words what she thinks of my figure, just to show you that not everyone is of your opinion! (*To Annette*) What did you say to me the other morning, precisely on the subject of my breasts?
Annette (*opening her eyes with difficulty*) I dode rebebber, Badarb.
Yvonne (*marking each point with a little tap on Annette's arms or chest*) Yes, you do! I was washing myself, and I said to you: "I don't care if I do say so myself, there are not many others who could boast a pair as firm as those!" And you said—what did you say?
Annette (*making an effort*) Oh, yes! I said: "It's true, Badarb, coppared with dose, bide are like two sacks of potatoes!"
Yvonne (*to Lucien*) There! You hear!
Lucien (*taking Annette roughly by the right arm and pushing her aside*) Well, what does that prove? I have never denied that you have beautiful breasts, but between beauty and perfection there is still a gulf.

Annette, awaiting the end of what seems likely to be a prolonged debate, goes to sit and doze off in the armchair near the fireplace

Yvonne Oh, really! Well, from now on, you can say goodbye to my breasts!

Lucien (*stretching out one hand in reply*) Oh, yes? Well . . .

Yvonne (*mistaking his intentions and tapping his hand*) Don't touch!

Lucien (*furiously*) I see!

Yvonne I shall save them for others, who know how to appreciate them! (*She reaches* DR *and climbs back into bed*)

Lucien (*furiously, pacing up and down with both hands in his trouser pockets*) Well! Well! That's a fine way to talk! Save them for others! Save them for who you like! For the Pope, if you want! No, no no! I've been patient up to now, but really!

Without looking, Lucien throws himself down on the chair near the fireplace that he thought was empty but on which Annette is asleep

Annette (*awoken suddenly and uttering a loud shriek*) Ah!

Lucien (*jumping back, astonished*) Eh! Are you asleep there, Annette?

Annette (*grumbling as she gets up*) Is dat all you god be up for?

Lucien (DS *of the bed*) It wasn't I who woke you up, it was Madame.

Annette You could have let be sleep!

Yvonne It's a good thing, isn't it, Annette, that we're not asking for your opinion . . . But as you're up——

Annette, who had already started to withdraw, stops at the sound of Yvonne's voice

——you may as well take the opportunity to go upstairs and let my husband have his bed back.

Annette starts to leave the room again, but stops as before at the sound of Lucien's voice

Lucien (*imperiously*) Not at all! Not at all! She has taken it, let her keep it! I shall sleep here.

Yvonne With me? Oh, no!

Lucien Yes, certainly! You can sleep where you like, but this is the marital bed, and I have the right to sleep in it!

Yvonne All right! But you know, if you're hoping to . . . you can think again!

Lucien (*with a shrug of the shoulders*) Oh, as for that! Wait till you're asked! (*He goes* US *of the bed and sits on the side, with his back to the audience, while he pulls off his shoes*)
Yvonne (*arranging the bedspread*) Yes, well! That's all right, then!

Annette tries to sleep upright against the doorpost of the room L

Lucien (*brusquely to her*) What's the matter with you?
Annette It's the biddle of the dight!
Lucien The biddle of the dight? The biddle of the dight!
Annette It's dot fuddy.
Lucien Well, you can go to bed now!
Annette (*with an aggrieved air*) Yes, sir!

Annette exits, shrugging her shoulders

Yvonne (*still grumbling*) Oh, no, it's too much! If you think you can go out and get excited looking at other women, and then come home and expect me to . . . ! Oh, no! I'm not going to play second fiddle.
Lucien (*exasperated*) Oh, please! Save all that for tomorrow; I'm tired.
Yvonne (*snuggling under the bedclothes, facing front, with her back to Lucien*) Oh, you're right! There's no point in discussing it; I'd rather go to sleep.
Lucien Well, then! That's that! Go to sleep!
Yvonne (*after a moment, half sitting up and over her shoulder*) All the same, I'm not sorry the maid was there to put you right.
Lucien (*undressing, furiously, waving his slipper with his right hand towards the door at the back*) Listen! Are you trying to drive me out again?
Yvonne (*lying back on her pillow, indifferently*) Do whatever you want.
Lucien (*exasperated, pacing up and down, one foot slippered and the other bare, which gives him a drunken gait*) Oh! Oh! Oh! (*He returns to the foot of the bed*) In the first place, what does she know about it, the maid? (*He tries to put his slipper on without sitting down*) If it comes to a comparison between her breasts and yours, it's obvious that, between the two, I would choose yours!

Yvonne (*sitting up abruptly*) So you want an expert opinion, is that it? Fine! Tomorrow night we have the manager of the perfume department of the Galeries Lafayette and Monsieur Godot coming to dinner; I'll show them my bosom, and we'll let them decide!

Lucien (*scandalized*) You're mad!

Yvonne Why? You said yourself that it was not improper.

Lucien (*forcefully*) It's not improper for someone who's completely naked!

Yvonne (*giving tit for tat*) Very well! I'll take all my clothes off!

Lucien (*stunned, appealing to the ceiling*) She's crazy! She's completely crazy!

Yvonne (*snuggling back under the covers*) Like a coat-hanger, am I? We shall see!

Lucien (*going to the foot of the bed, clasping his hands*) Ah, no, please! Please! You're driving me mad with your tomfoolery! (*He moves* US *between the hall door and the desk*)

Yvonne (*half-rising, scornfully*) Well, well! Come to bed then, what are you waiting for? You're not planning to stay dressed up as the Sun King all night, are you?

Lucien (*faintly, pressing his fingers against his stomach*) No.

Yvonne (*looking at him with pity, in a tone of concern*) What's the matter now?

Lucien (*miserably*) I've got stomach ache.

Yvonne Oh, come on! Cheer up! (*She throws back the covers and jumps out of bed*)

Lucien Perhaps Annette could make me some camomile.

Yvonne (*putting on her slippers*) All right! (*She moves across towards the door*) We'll make you some camomile!

Lucien (*standing in her way*) But you don't have to get up. I can do it myself.

Yvonne (*pushing him back*) Oh, no! (*She turns on him*) I don't want you to be able to say that I let you suffer! No! I know my duty! And I shall do it!

Lucien (*in the same tone*) Good! That's all right then!

Yvonne (*going to the door* L *and calling*) Annette!

Annette (*off*) Oh!

Yvonne Get up, Annette!

Annette (*off*) What! Agaid!

Yvonne What do you mean, "Agaid?" Certainly, "Again!" Get up and make some camomile for the master. (*She goes to the mantelpiece and taking the box of matches strikes one to light the tea-maker*)

Annette can be heard grumbling off stage

Lucien (*after a moment, sniggering*) Ah, no! Now you've really annoyed that girl!

Yvonne, the box of matches in one hand, a match in the other, turns round at this remark

Yvonne Oh, that's the last straw! So it's me who's upset her! (*She goes to Lucien, close to his face*) Tell me then . . . Is it for me, the camomile, eh, is it for me?

Lucien (*close to tears*) It's my supper that has not gone down!

Yvonne Oh, yes! it's always the same story! (*She returns to the mantelpiece to prepare the tea, lighting the wick and pouring water from the carafe into the receptacle*) That's what it all comes down to: over-eating and indigestion! Your wife isn't sufficiently attractive for you to stay at home, but she's good enough to look after you when you're not well!

Lucien has not heard a word of this diatribe, being preoccupied with his stomach ache, which he tries to alleviate by pressing his fingers against the bottom of his ribs. He now comes behind Yvonne

Lucien What did you say, my dear?

Yvonne (*without turning round*) What?

Lucien (*pitifully*) Will it take long, the camomile?

Yvonne All in good time . . . it has to boil . . . you know that!

Lucien (*resigned*) Yes. (*After a moment he hiccoughs, then in a doleful voice*) Ah!

Yvonne (*half turning*) Now what?

Lucien (*half leaning on her, miserably*) I should like to be sick!

Yvonne (*pushing Lucien away hurriedly and crossing in front of him*) Ah, no! you're not going to be sick! I didn't marry you for that!

Lucien No, no! I said, "I would like to be", not "I'm going to be". You know very well that I never could.

Yvonne (*scornfully*) Ah, yes, I know! Poor thing! (*She returns to the bed and climbs into it*)

Annette appears with a packet of camomile and a sugar basin. She has put on a white camisole and her stockings which have, however, fallen down round her ankles. She puts the camomile into the hot water

Annette (*sulkily*) Is dere eddythig else while I'b here?
Yvonne (*sweetly, from the bed, arranging the bedclothes over herself*) Ask Monsieur, Annette! He is the one who is ill!
Lucien (*wearily*) I've got stomach ache.
Annette (*equally weary, without turning round*) I'b dot surprised! If Bodsieur is goig to bake a poppyshow of hibself outside!
Lucien (*flying off the handle*) Oh, no! No! You're not going to start sticking your oar in!
Annette (*indifferently*) Oh, it's duthig to be!

Yvonne starts to get out of bed

Lucien Yes, well . . . (*To Yvonne*) Get back to bed!
Annette (*not needing to be told twice*) I'b goig, I'b goig!
Lucien (*to Annette*) Oh, no!
Annette Oh, yes!

Annette exits

Lucien (*furiously*) I was speaking to Madame! (*To Yvonne*) It's too bad . . . when even the servants start to meddle!
Yvonne (*with a pinched smile*) All the same, there was no need to bite her head off like that. She was quite right; if you hadn't bolted your supper . . .
Lucien Quite possibly! But that's none of her business! I'm not answerable to the servants! (*He sits on the bench*) I had supper because I felt like it, so there! And because I was with Monsieur Godot and the Espink brothers who felt hungry and wanted something to eat; is that a crime?
Yvonne No, it's not a crime! Obviously, it's not a crime! But it's idiotic to eat something that gives you indigestion! This passion for food! (*A long silence. Then in an icy tone*) Who paid?
Lucien (*shrugging his shoulders*) No-one!
Yvonne What do you mean, "No-one"?
Lucien All right then, everyone; we each paid for our own.

Yvonne I'm surprised it wasn't you who paid, with your mania for showing off!

Lucien Me!

Yvonne Yes, you! You're stingy with the housekeeping! But the moment you're out with your friends, you swagger about like a millionaire!

Lucien (*getting up and coming* DS) Me! Swagger about! What makes you think that?

Yvonne (*topping his reply*) You've only to look in the mirror! Look at you now! Who do you decide to dress up as? The Sun King! I ask you! You dress up as the Sun King . . . and it rains! You look ridiculous!

Lucien (*sitting on the chair beside the desk*) You're the one who's being ridiculous!

Yvonne (*not going to let him off the hook*) It's only because it flatters you to strut about as Louis the Fifteenth.

Lucien throws a supercilious glance at her and shrugs his shoulders

Lucien (*calmly*) Fourteenth!

Yvonne What do you mean, "Fourteenth"?

Lucien The Sun King was Louis the Fourteenth.

Yvonne (*taken aback*) Ah? (*She sits up*) Oh well, all right then, Louis the Fourteenth! (*Brusquely*) That's just like you—to quibble about one Louis and then, when it's a question of your own pleasure, the sky's the limit.

Lucien (*getting up and making a semi-circle down towards the bench*) Oh, charming! Delightful!

Yvonne (*after a moment, in the same icy tone*) How much did you spend on your supper?

Lucien (*with an impatient gesture*) How do I know?

Yvonne (*getting up on to her knees on the bed*) You don't even know how much you spent?

Lucien (*raising his eyes heavenwards*) Eleven francs, sixty-five, then!

Yvonne (*raising herself as high as she can on her knees and grasping the rail at the bottom of the bed with both hands*) You spent eleven francs, sixty-five, on a blow-out! There you are, just as I said! (*She changes her tone*) The other day . . .

Lucien senses that battle is about to be rejoined on new and dangerous ground. He shakes his head nervously and swears under his breath. He moves US

Yvonne (*pursuing her advantage and jumping off the bed*) What a pig! (*She joins Lucien and turns him by the arms to face her*) The other day, when I had the misfortune to buy a bottle of Rose-Coty, you said I would be the ruin of you; and then you spend eleven francs, sixty-five, on your supper! But me, at least I have my perfume to show for it, my Rose-Coty, while you, your supper, where is it now?

Lucien (*enraged, patting his stomach*) In here, in here! (*He sits down on the chair next to the desk*)

Yvonne (*returning to the bed and climbing back into it*) Ah! In there, in there! You're pleased with yourself, aren't you? But you would have done better to put those eleven francs, sixty-five, aside . . . to pay the decorator's bill!

Lucien I owe him eight hundred francs; can you see me offering him eleven francs, sixty-five!

Yvonne It would have shown good faith, at least! Speaking of which, he's coming to see you today.

Lucien (*pricking up his ears*) Ah!

Yvonne He says he has had enough of being fobbed off . . . and that if you don't give him a substantial payment on account, he has decided to issue a writ; he'll have a summons served on you at the Galeries Lafayette! You can imagine what kind of an impression that will make.

Lucien (*getting up and moving* DS) He said that?

Yvonne Yes.

Lucien But that's blackmail! (*He speaks in the direction of the hall door, as if to the decorator*) A fine way to behave! (*To Yvonne*) And just as I was reckoning on settling his bill . . .

Yvonne (*implacably*) When?

Lucien (*taken aback*) Eh! When I could! But since it's like that, he can whistle for it!

Yvonne (*hammering every word, with her hands in the air*) And you go and spend eleven francs, sixty-five, on your supper!

Lucien has returned US *of the bed. He loses his temper*

Lucien Ah no! I don't want to hear any more about my supper!

Yvonne (*relentlessly*) No, really, in your place, I shouldn't have the stomach for it either!
Lucien (*thrusting his face into hers*) But I have! That's what annoys you, isn't it? I've eaten it!
Yvonne (*as loudly as him*) There's no need to shout! I'm fed up with it! You're wearing me out with your wrangling!
Lucien (*moving away* DS) Ah, no! That takes the cake! So it's *my* wrangling now, is it? When I'm the one who is worn out!
Yvonne Do you want to go to sleep or not?
Lucien (*returning above the bed*) Oh, yes, sleep, sleep! I'm dropping on my feet!
Yvonne (*turning her back on him and disappearing under the bed clothes*) Good! So am I! Good-night!
Lucien Good-night!
Yvonne (*a final dismissal*) Good-night!
Lucien (*sitting on the end of the bed, equally firmly*) Good-night!

Lucien sits on the bed and on Yvonne's ankle. She gives him a kick through the bed-clothes

Yvonne Mind my foot!
Lucien (*getting up; furiously*) Mind your foot! (*He puts his left foot on the rail at the end of the bed, in order to raise his knee so that he can reach to take off the garters on his trousers*) Oh! Go to sleep! (*He takes off the garter*) There's no need to kick me like that!

After a moment a bell rings in the hall

Lucien and Yvonne freeze. The bell rings again. Yvonne lifts her head slowly and, half-rising, looks anxiously at Lucien. Lucien slowly takes his foot off the bed-rail and going round to the L *throws an interrogatory glance at Yvonne*

Yvonne (*whispering*) What's that?
Lucien (*also whispering*) I don't know! It must be the front door.

Another ring on the bell makes them jump

Yvonne (*sitting up straight*) Oh, my God!
Lucien It can't be a visitor.
Yvonne For anyone to come at this time of night, it must be something serious.

Lucien (*panic-stricken*) Yes.

The bell rings again

Yvonne (*jumping out of bed and putting on her slippers*) There it is again! Oh, Lucien, Lucien, I'm frightened . . . (*She snatches up her robe from the foot of the bed*)

Lucien (*equally alarmed*) Go on! Hurry up! Answer it! We can't just let it ring!

Yvonne (*demented, going from one side of the room to the other, as if searching for something*) Ah, it's easy for you! You're a man, but as for me . . .

The bell rings

Oh!

Lucien (*turning and re-turning on the same spot*) It's bad news! It must be!

Yvonne But where is it, where is it?

Lucien What?

Yvonne (*gesticulating frantically*) My robe! Where did I put my robe?

Lucien You're holding it!

Yvonne What? Oh! Yes!

The bell rings repeatedly

Lucien
Yvonne } (*together*) Oh!

Yvonne (*about to put on her robe but stopping*) Ah! This ringing will drive me mad!

Lucien (*indicating the room* L) Where's Annette? Why doesn't she answer it? (*He goes to her door*)

Yvonne (*giving up the idea of putting on her robe and running to join him*) Oh, that girl!

Lucien and Yvonne stand on the threshold of the door, with Lucien US *and Yvonne* DS

Lucien
Yvonne } (*together*) Annette! Annette!

Annette (*off*) Hoon!

Yvonne Quickly, get up!

Annette (*off*) Huh! Agaid!

Another ring

Yvonne Hurry up!
Lucien Can't you hear the bell?
Annette (*off; tearfully*) Ah! dough, dough! You expect too buch!
Yvonne (*moving to the bench*) Let's hope it's nothing to do with the family.
Lucien (*near the fireplace*) Of course not! You're frightening yourself over nothing.

Yvonne drops her robe quickly on the bed and grabs the bench on which she taps

Yvonne Touch wood! Touch wood!
Lucien You know very well that if it was really——
Yvonne Touch wood, I said!
Lucien (*bewildered*) Yes, but you know quite well that if——
Yvonne Touch wood, anyway!
Lucien Yes!

Absent-mindedly, to humour Yvonne, Lucien taps three times on the nearest surface within reach that happens to be the marble mantelpiece

Yvonne But not that, look, it's marble!
Lucien You've got me at it now! (*He goes to touch the desk*)
Yvonne With the palm of your hand!
Lucien (*obeying mechanically*) With the palm.
Yvonne You'll bring bad luck!

A prolonged ringing on the bell. Yvonne bounds towards the door L

What is she doing, that girl?
Lucien (*also going to the door*) You there, get a move on!

At this precise moment, Annette appears

Yvonne and Lucien each take an arm and propel her in front of them towards the hall. Annette repeatedly returns to them and each time is pushed back towards the door, so that she is spinning like a top

Annette Oh, dough! I've had eduff! Badarb doesn'd pay by wages . . . I wad to go hobe!

Lucien } *(together at the* } Yes, yes! Good! Go, then go!
Yvonne } *end of their patience)*

Annette I'b dot doig eddy bore!

Ringing. The following speeches overlap

Lucien Will you go and open the door, blockhead!
Yvonne Go on, hurry up!
Annette (*as she is being pushed towards the hall*) Yes, bud subwud has to pay by wages!
Lucien Call yourself a maid!

Annette exits

Lucien is R and Yvonne L of the hall door

Annette (*in the hall*) Who is it?
Joseph (*off; distantly*) Joseph! I am the new manservant of Madame's mother.
Yvonne (*shrieking*) Mama! Something has happened to Mama! Something has happened to Mama!
Lucien Don't cry like that, my dear, don't cry!

During the following exchange, there is the sound of the safety chain being taken off and the front door opened

Yvonne (*shrieking*) Mama! Something has happened to Mama! Something has happened to Mama!
Lucien Don't cry like that, my dear, don't cry!

Joseph appears

Yvonne grabs hold of him and drags him DS to C. Joseph is wearing a suit with a woollen scarf round his neck, and he carries a bowler hat in his hand

Annette enters shortly after Joseph. She has had time to close the front door and replace the safety chain. She comes down near the fireplace

Yvonne (*before Joseph has had time to speak*) What has happened to Mama? What has happened to Mama?
Joseph (*very embarrassed, with his head bowed*) Oh, Madame . . .

In his discomfort, turning his head from side to side, he finds himself looking at the feet of Lucien, whom he did not have a chance to see on first coming into the room. His glance travels first up Lucien's legs, with gathering astonishment up Lucien's body, and he is then unable to repress a cry of surprise when confronted with the full sight of this man dressed up as Louis XIV

Ah!

Lucien (*with an instinctive glance down at his own costume*) What, what is it? Tell us, instead of staring at my outfit! it's nothing unusual.

Yvonne (*to Joseph*) An accident?

Joseph (*his head low again, twisting his hat mechanically between his hands, quickly*) Oh! no . . .

Yvonne (*relieved*) Ah!

Lucien There, you see, no accident!

Joseph (*hesitating*) Only . . . she's not well . . .

Yvonne (*anguished*) Mama is not well? Why? What's the matter?

Joseph Well, she is ill.

Yvonne (*hardly daring to ask*) Oh, my God! Seriously?

Joseph Well . . . rather!

Yvonne (*crossing* R *to take refuge in Lucien's arms*) Lucien! Lucien! Mama is ill!

Lucien Oh, come on now!

Yvonne Mama is very ill!

Lucien Wait a minute!

Joseph (*moving away* L) And when I say very ill, that's a manner of speaking; because, to tell the truth, she is really . . . she is really . . .

Yvonne (*following him to* C, *a lump in her throat*) What? What? What is she really?

Joseph She is really . . . (*turning to her and lifting his head, abruptly*) dead!

All Ah!

Yvonne faints, but is caught by Lucien, who has followed her to C

Lucien (*sitting quickly on the floor, with Yvonne in his arms*) Ah! That's what I was afraid of.

Joseph (*once this scene is complete*) Only . . . they advised me to break the news gently to Madame, so as not to upset her. (*Aside, with a long sigh of relief*) Ouf!

Lucien What a catastrophe! And just as we were going to bed!

Annette (*beside herself*) Badarb! Badarb!

Lucien A fine mess you made of things, telling her like that!

Joseph But, sir, they told me . . .

Lucien Do you call that breaking it gently! Well, you'd better help me now.

Joseph Yes, sir. (*He places his hat on the desk, then kneels behind Yvonne while Lucien moves down between Yvonne and the bench*)

Annette (*near the fireplace*) Oh, by God!

Lucien steps over Yvonne to go to Annette and then pushes her towards the door L

Lucien (*to Annette*) And you, go and find the smelling salts and some vinegar, instead of crying. That won't do any good!

Annette Yes, sir. Oh, by God!

Annette exits

Joseph, during this time, in order to support Yvonne, has passed his forearms under her armpits and has his hands pressed firmly against her breasts

Joseph If we could just lift Madame . . . on to the bed!

In saying "on to the bed" he marks each syllable with a jerk of the wrists towards the bed, which causes Yvonne's breasts to wobble with every word

Lucien (*returning to Joseph*) Eh? Yes . . . (*He notices Joseph's position and throws himself towards him*) But what do you think you're doing!

Joseph (*still holding Yvonne, who wobbles slightly as before*) I'm holding her up.

Lucien (*trying to push Joseph aside to take his place*) But what a way of holding her! Can't you see that she is not wearing corsets?

Joseph (*without letting go*) Oh, Monsieur! As if I should think of such a thing!

Lucien (*on his knees to the left of Yvonne*) I don't care whether you think about it or not! I'm telling you to let go! (*He pushes*

Joseph aside and passes, always on his knees, to Yvonne's right) Now look and see if there isn't a small bottle of ether, over there, near the bed.
Joseph (*going to search* US *of the bed*) Yes, sir, yes! (*He clambers across the bed to reach the other side*)
Lucien Mind the bedclothes! Mind the bedclothes!
Joseph (*who has uncorked the bottle and sniffed the contents*) This is it, Monsieur.
Lucien Good; give it here.

Joseph brings it to Lucien

Yvonne! my darling! Yvonne! (*To Joseph*) Now we need some linen. Find me some linen, to make a swab.
Joseph (*looking left and right like a weathercock, not knowing which way to turn*) Linen? Linen? Where is there any?
Lucien (*pulling the cork from the medicine bottle with his teeth*) I don't know! If I knew, I wouldn't ask you! Look for some!

Joseph catches sight of the petticoat hanging over the back of the chair L *and steps over Yvonne's legs to reach it*

Joseph Here we are. (*He picks up the petticoat*) Will this do?
Lucien (*murmuring, gently shaking Yvonne*) Yvonne! Darling! (*To Joseph*) I don't know! What is it?
Joseph (*bringing it to him*) It looks like a petticoat!
Lucien (*with the cork between his teeth*) That's better than nothing! All right, kneel down!

Joseph obeys

Now roll that into a swab. You know what a swab is?
Joseph Yes, sir. (*He rolls the petticoat into a swab*)
Lucien That's fine, give it to me (*He holds the bottle of ether out to Joseph*) Take that!

Joseph, on his knees on the other side of Yvonne, takes the bottle from Lucien and passes him the petticoat in exchange

(*With the cork in his mouth*) Cork! Cork!

Joseph looks all over the floor for the cork

Here! Here! In my mouth!

Joseph retrieves the cork from Lucien's lips

Good! Ether! Ether!

Lucien holds out the swab to Joseph, who impregnates it with ether. Lucien dab's Yvonne's face with it

Yvonne! Darling! (*To Joseph, holding out the swab for him to pour a little more ether on it*) Ah, frankly, you know, you ... (*To Yvonne*) Yvonne! Yvonne! (*To Joseph*) You should have waited until tomorrow to come and break such news to us!

Joseph If Monsieur thinks it was pleasant for me!

Lucien No, but it would have been more pleasant for us! (*To Yvonne*) Yvonne, my darling! (*To Joseph*) I ask you, what was the hurry? Obviously, my poor mother-in-law, it's a great misfortune! But what difference would a few hours have made? She wasn't going to fly away! And, at least, Madame would have been spared a troubled night ... (*a semi-tone lower*) and so should I!

Joseph I'm sorry, sir! The next time I'll know better.

Annette rushes in with a salt-cellar and a large cut-glass vinegar bottle which, passing in front of Joseph, she thrusts into Lucien's face

Annette Here you are, sir!

Lucien lifts his head, looks at the salt-cellar, looks at Annette, looks again at the salt-cellar

Lucien What's that?
Annette Id's the salt-cellar.
Lucien What do you want me to do with it?
Annette It was you that asked be for salt.
Lucien For smelling-salts, dunderhead, not salt! Do you think I'm going to pickle Madame?
Annette How do I dough? I'b dot a doctor.

Yvonne starts to come round

Lucien Ah, good! Madame has opened her eyes! Wait! Stand back! And take that away!

Lucien gives the petticoat to Joseph, who gets up and moves away, to stand with Annette US *of the fireplace. Mechanically, during what follows, without letting the audience see, Joseph stuffs the petticoat into his coat pocket. Lucien slides behind Yvonne and sits against her on the floor with his limbs parallel to the front of the stage, so that his feet emerge to the right of Yvonne and his body to her left*

Lucien Yvonne! Yvonne!
Yvonne (*looking left and right as she regains her senses*) What has happened?
Lucien Nothing, my dear, nothing at all!
Yvonne But why am I on the floor? (*Her gaze falls on Joseph*) Oh! Yes! Now I remember! Mama! My poor Mama! (*She bursts out sobbing on Lucien's chest*)
Lucien (*taking her in his arms and rocking her gently like a baby*) There, there! There, there! Steady now! There, there! (*A touch of asperity creeps in*) Oh, for God's sake! (*Soothing again*) There, there!
Annette Oh, my God!
Lucien Come on now! Cheer up! Don't give up hope!
Yvonne (*sobbing with mortification*) How can there be hope when she's dead?
Lucien Well then! Just so! The worst is over! Dash it, look on the bright side! Think of it as a deliverance! Remember how your poor Mama used to suffer from rheumatism!
Yvonne (*sobbing*) Poor Mama!
Lucien (*sadly and tenderly*) There you are then, there you are! Now she is no longer suffering! While we are here (*with a hint of rancour*) awake and crying for her, she is asleep! She can rest, happy!
Yvonne (*nodding her head sadly*) Who would have thought that she would go so fast!
Lucien Ah, yes! When I was asking myself just now how I was going to pay the decorator, I little thought that . . . well, well!
Yvonne (*sobbing*) My poor Mama!
Lucien Ah, yes! Your poor, brave, worthy saint of a mother! (*Aside*) My back's aching! (*While speaking, finding his position uncomfortable, he gets first to his knees, then arches his aching back, looks round left and right for a chair that he might pull towards him, then, tenderly*) Tell me, Yvonne!
Yvonne What?
Lucien Wouldn't you like to sit down, my sweetheart?

Yvonne (*suddenly, shouting with a vehemence that startles Lucien*) Oh, no! Sit down! What does it matter whether I'm sitting on a chair or on the ground?
Lucien (*quickly*) Yes, yes! Good! (*He goes to sit on the bench*)
Yvonne (*waxing lyrical in her grief*) It's *under* the ground that I'd like to be!
Annette (*near the fireplace, sorrowfully*) Oh, it will be the death of you, Badarb!
Yvonne (*sobbing and grimacing, as if her face is stiff, to Lucien*) What is this? (*To Joseph*) Why is my face sticky?
Lucien It's nothing, my dear! Just ether.
Yvonne What sort of ether?
Joseph (*indicating the table by the bed*) That was in the bottle there.
Yvonne But that is syrup of ether, my medicine! Why did you put it on my face?
Lucien Syrup!
Joseph (*taking the bottle from his pocket and hastily glancing at the label*) Oh, I didn't read the label! I just smelt it.

Joseph gives the bottle to Annette, who puts it on the mantelpiece

Lucien Oh, you're a smart fellow-my-lad and no mistake!
Yvonne (*lyrical again*) Anyway, what does it matter! When one's heart (*grimace*) is in a thousand pieces! (*Another grimace. Then, to Annette*) Oh, get me some hot water, please, Annette, so that I can wash it off.
Annette Yes, Badarb.

She exits UR *through the archway*

Yvonne (*with a sad tenderness*) The poor dear woman! Do you remember how good she was?
Lucien (*nodding distractedly, then*) Who?
Yvonne (*slapping his leg*) Mama, of course!
Lucien Ah, yes!
Yvonne And so indulgent towards you! Always making excuses for you! When I think how you treated her, how you used to abuse her! It's only two days ago that you went so far as to call her a cow!
Lucien (*beseeching her to stop*) Yvonne!
Yvonne (*tearfully*) How could you have called her a cow?

Lucien gives a vague gesture as he searches for an excuse, then, as if it were the best reason, in the world:

Lucien I didn't know she was going to die!
Yvonne Then that must be your punishment.
Lucien (*turning* US *on the bench*) Oh, Lord! (*He stays with his back to the audience, head in hand, elbow on the bed-rail, throughout the following*)
Yvonne To think that she has gone to her grave with that memory of your lack of respect! Cow! My saintly mother! (*She settles into a low, slow, rhythmic tone*)

Lucien gives the impression of nodding his agreement at the end of each phrase, though in reality he is dropping off to sleep

Ah, well! You will have to live with that! I know better than anyone what a wealth of generosity there was in Mama's heart; and I believe I am interpreting her feelings aright in saying that her final message to you would have been: "Go in peace, Lucien! I forgive you!" (*Repeating sadly*) "I forgive . . ."

Receiving no response Yvonne looks up and sees that Lucien has dozed off while she has been speaking. She gives him a vigorous tap on the calf

You're asleep!
Lucien (*waking with a start*) Hein! Me? What . . . .! Ah! I'm sorry! A little tired!
Yvonne (*indignantly*) Tired! Mama is dead and he's tired!

Yvonne jumps up and, grabbing Lucien, she sends him cannoning into Joseph's stomach

Lucien⎫
Joseph⎬ (*together*) Oh!

Yvonne Shouldn't we be going?
Lucien Ah! You feel that we should go? . . .
Yvonne Of course we must! You didn't think we were going back to bed?
Lucien (*sighing, as he throws a wistful glance at the bed*) No!

Yvonne pushes Lucien briskly out of her way towards C *as she moves over to the armchair* L. *She picks up her vest from the chair and then puts it back*

My petticoat? Where is my petticoat? (*She pushes Joseph aside towards the fireplace and moves up to the chair next to the desk*)
Lucien (*to Joseph*) But I gave it to you!
Joseph To me!
Lucien To you!
Joseph Ah, yes! (*Pulling the petticoat slowly from his pocket*) Here it is, Madame.
Yvonne (*having returned between them, to Joseph*) What were you doing with my petticoat in your pocket?
Joseph Your husband was using it . . . to put the syrup on your face, Madame.
Yvonne (*snatching the petticoat from him*) You must have been crazy, the pair of you!

Yvonne returns to Lucien, who is rooted to the spot, as if waiting for the next blow to fall

Well, stir yourself! Why aren't you getting dressed?
Lucien Ah? Dressed?
Yvonne (*exasperated*) Of course! You weren't thinking of going down there as Louis the Fourteenth?
Lucien No!
Yvonne (*to Joseph*) Dressing up as Louis the Fourteenth when he has lost his mother-in-law!
Joseph (*laughing without thinking*) Ha! ha!
Yvonne (*coldly*) You think it's funny, do you?
Joseph Oh! Pardon, no!

Annette enters from the bathroom

Lucien (*to Annette*) Ah! Annette! Fetch me my black suit, black tie and black gloves.

Annette is moving towards the door of the room L, *when she is stopped by Yvonne's voice*

Yvonne (*turning her husband to face her, exasperated*) Ah, no! No! You can't go dressed like that! You'll look as though you had ordered your mourning clothes in advance; that won't do! (*She crosses and drops her petticoat on the end of the bed*)

Lucien You're right! (*He goes to Annette*) Very well! Whatever suit you want, Annette, my . . . my brightest one!
Annette Yes, sir.

Annette goes out

Yvonne undoes the ribbons of her nightdress, preparatory to taking it off before putting on her petticoat

Yvonne (*grumbling*) Nobody would believe it!

Yvonne is facing the foot of the bed and so has her back to Joseph, who is watching this scene with an air of studied indifference

Lucien (*going to Joseph*) As for you . . . (*He is struck by something in Joseph's attitude, he turns to see what he is looking at and bounds over to his wife, to lift up her nightdress just as it has started to slip from her shoulders*) What are you doing? Have you gone mad?
Yvonne (*startled by this bolt from the blue*) What?
Lucien You mean to take off your nightdress, here?
Yvonne (*nerves on edge*) Now listen to me! (*She throws the nightdress back, with the intention of slipping her arms out of the sleeves*)
Lucien (*pulling the nightdress up again*) No! You listen to me! You're not going to undress in front of the servant!
Joseph (*preserving his air of detachment*) Oh, don't mind me, sir!
Lucien (*furiously, thrusting his face into Joseph's*) But I *do* mind you!
Yvonne (*to Joseph, with Lucien between them*) No! But I've just lost my mother: what does it matter whether I'm dressed or not! (*She moves away towards the bed*)
Lucien (*furiously*) It's possible to lose one's mother *and* be respectable!
Yvonne Oh, yes! Shut up, you! Get away from me!

Annette appears from L, *carrying on her arm a complete outfit for Lucien and holding in her other hand his shoes, on which is balanced his bowler hat. From the trousers, attached to buttons at the back but not the front, dangle Lucien's braces*

Yvonne Come here, Annette! Come and help me get ready!

Yvonne exits through the archway R, carrying her robe and petticoat

Annette deposits Lucien's clothes on the chair L, his shoes on the floor and his hat over one of the candlesticks on the mantelpiece

Lucien What a night! My God, what a night!
Joseph Luckily, sir, it doesn't happen every day!
Lucien Ah! You think it's all a joke, don't you! (*To Annette*) See here, my girl! I don't know what belongs to what! You'll have to help me.
Annette (*with a much put upon air, as she goes towards the archway R*) But, sir, I have to help Badarb!
Lucien Go, then, go!

Annette goes out

Lucien moves to Joseph and taps him on the shoulder

Lucien You'll have to help me then.
Joseph Yes, sir.
Lucien You know what to do?
Joseph Yes, sir!
Lucien Good! Then let's get started.

Joseph moves vaguely US

Where are you going?
Joseph (*flustered*) I don't know, sir.
Lucien Oh! you're a bright spark, I can see that! After all that, I can't remember what I wanted to say to you! (*Suddenly*) Ah, yes! (*He moves US towards the desk*)

Joseph, attentively, without knowing why, moves US at the same time

What are you doing? I am going to write a letter; I don't need you for that.
Joseph Oh! Pardon!
Lucien That's all right. (*He takes the chair from beside the desk, puts it in front of the desk and, sitting down, starts to write*)
Joseph (*after a moment, moving L of desk, near Lucien*) I must say I felt pretty small, sir, coming here as I did . . . It's the first time I've had the honour of meeting you and your wife, and in such circumstances! Honestly, I wish I'd had the job of

telling you that you had won top prize in a lottery, rather than the news I had.

Lucien, without interrupting his writing, makes a sign with his left hand to Joseph, to stop him talking. But Joseph takes no notice

It was a weight off my mind when I had told you! But honestly, I wouldn't want to go through all that again!

Lucien (*still writing*) You're stopping me from writing.

Joseph I'm sorry, sir. (*With his hands behind his back and his hat in his hands, he comes down near to the foot of the bed*)

Lucien Annette! (*He moistens the edge of one of the letter-cards he has just written*) Annette!

Joseph (*glancing at Lucien, then moving complacently up to the archway* R *and standing in it*) Mademoiselle, Monsieur is calling you!

Annette (*off*) I ab dressig Badarb, Bodsieur.

Yvonne (*off*) You can go in a minute.

Lucien (*sealing a second letter-card*) Yes, yes!

Joseph (*still in the archway, with his gaze focussed firmly on the interior of the offstage bathroom*) She won't be long, sir! Madame has her petticoat on now!

Lucien slams the desk shut and launches himself on Joseph, sending him spinning to the centre of the stage

Lucien That's quite enough of that! There's no need for you to stick your nose into everything!

Joseph (*taken aback by this failure to appreciate his services*) It was only to oblige you, sir!

Lucien Oblige me! Oblige me! Well, you can oblige me by shutting up and helping me with my clothes.

Joseph looks round helplessly

My clothes! There! There! (*He pushes Joseph* L) Go on! Now take them over there! (*He pushes him over towards the bed*)

Joseph Yes, sir.

Lucien And help me!

Joseph Yes, sir.

During the following, Joseph takes Lucien's cloak, then unfastens his jerkin. Underneath, Lucien is wearing a shirt with a collar and tie. This all takes place at the foot of the bed, near the bench

Lucien (*undressing*) Tell me, have you got a cab waiting downstairs?

Joseph Yes, sir.

Lucien Hurry up, then! We musn't keep it waiting too long.

Joseph Especially as it's a taxi. (*He finishes unfastening Lucien and is now on his left*)

Lucien (*going* US *of the bed*) Though, after all, what does it matter? It's not every day we have something to celebrate!

Joseph (*scandalised*) Celebrate!

Lucien Huh? No! What! You don't understand! (*He takes his trousers and put them on without thinking over his Louis XIV breeches*)

Annette enters from the bathroom and passes Lucien, who is dressing with his back to the audience. She stops just to his left

Annette Bodsieur deeds be?

Lucien (*dressing himself*) Madame is ready?

Annette Sood!

Lucien So what do you want?

Annette To dough if you deed be, sir?

Lucien No!

Annette moves to go

Yes!

Annette stops

Wait, my girl. (*He dresses as he speaks with the absent-minded air of someone trying to do two things at once*) There are two . . . two letters on the . . .

Joseph moves officiously towards the desk with the intention of making himself useful

(*To Joseph*) Not you! (*To Annette*) You, blockhead! Don't you understand? They're on the desk? They're on the desk! Take them downstairs and put them in the post.

Annette (*rebelliously*) Dow?

Lucien Of course, now! They must be delivered by first post tomorrow.

Annette (*sullenly*) Dat's all very well! (*She moves towards the door* L)

Joseph meanwhile has moved down to the fireplace

Lucien (*putting on his waistcoat and jacket without noticing that his braces are hanging down from the buttons at the back of his trousers*) Where are you going? Where are you going?
Annette I'b goig to put od by skirt!
Lucien Your skirt! Who do you think is going to take any notice of you at five o'clock in the morning!
Annette I card go out like dis id by petticoat! Id's dot right.
Lucien Well, take a waterproof.
Annette I have'd got a waterproof.
Lucien You can take mine: it's hanging in the hall.
Annette I card wear dat! Id's dot right!
Lucien That will do very well: now be off with you!
Annette It'll bake be look like a wobad of the streets!
Lucien Well, if anyone tries to pick you up, come and tell me about it!
Annette Who'd believe be!

She goes out sulkily into the hall

Lucien (*dressed, his braces hanging down behind, to Joseph*) There! Give me my . . . give me my . . .

Joseph turns left and then right, not knowing what he is looking for, then raises his eyes to the ceiling

My shoes! They're not on the ceiling!

Lucien picks up the shoes himself and sits on the bench to put them on

You're not very bright, are you?
Joseph Monsieur didn't explain himself.
Lucien Oh, well! Come here!

Joseph drops on his knees in front of Lucien to help him, and picks up the shoe that Lucien has not already taken. Lucien then snatches it from him

Give it to me! That'll do! (*He puts on his shoes*)

Joseph moves up towards the desk

Tell me, what sort of taxi have you got downstairs?
Joseph A Renault.

Lucien A little red one? Ah, that's good! The fastest and the cheapest.

Joseph At this time of night, I was lucky to find it.

Lucien Yes, it was a stroke of luck! That's all one can say, we're in luck!

Yvonne comes out of the bathroom, a large cloak over her robe and her head enveloped in a silk scarf

Joseph moves to the desk

Yvonne Well! Are you ready?

Lucien Yes, right away! (*He crosses* DL *to the fireplace*)

Yvonne (*to Joseph*) Have you got a car?

Joseph Yes, Madame, downstairs.

Lucien (*taking his hat from the mantelpiece*) A Renault! A little red one; the fastest and the cheapest. (*He puts on his hat without realizing that he is still wearing his wig and goes to join his wife* US) There! I'm ready.

Yvonne (*turning round and looking at him*) What about your wig! You're not going out with your wig on, are you?

Lucien Huh! My wig . . . You're confusing me! I don't know what I'm doing! (*He takes the wig off and puts it on the mantelpiece*)

Yvonne Oh, my God! Now that we've come to it, I'm frightened to think what we shall find when we get there.

Lucien (*returning to her*) Yes! Fate can play cruel tricks on you sometimes; but you know what they say—it's an ill wind . . .

Lucien passes Yvonne and exits into the hall

Yvonne takes Joseph by the arm and leads him DS

Lucien is stopped by the sound of his wife's voice and returns to follow them

Yvonne Tell me . . .

Joseph Madame?

Yvonne She is not too changed, at the last?

Joseph Oh, no, not at all.

Yvonne Poor Mama! Tell me that she did not suffer too much.

Lucien, perceiving that this could take a long time, drops into the armchair near the fireplace

Joseph (*happy to give Yvonne this consolation*) Not for an instant! She was in excellent spirits . . . She ate a good dinner: two slices of lamb . . .
Yvonne (*with emotion, eyes to heaven*) Two slices of lamb!
Lucien (*in distress, a reminder of his own troubles*) Two slices of lamb!
Joseph (*sighing in sympathy*) Two slices of lamb, yes! (*He resumes his tale*) After dinner, she played two or three games of patience; then she went up to bed . . . with Monsieur.
Yvonne (*prostrate with grief, barely audible*) My poor Mama . . . (*Only now do the final words of Joseph penetrate: she raises her head slowly with a questioning look and turns her head towards him*)
Yvonne
Lucien } (*together*) Monsieur?
Yvonne Mama went to bed with a man?
Lucien (*rising*) What man?
Joseph (*with a slight note of uncertainty creeping into his voice*) Why . . . Monsieur Fajolet! Madame's father!
Yvonne My father!

Lucien with teeth gritted and chin forward, advances on Joseph and making him turn round with a smart tap on the arm

Lucien What do you mean, her father? Who is this man? My mother-in-law is a widow!
Joseph (*recoiling* US) A widow! Then you're not Monsieur and Madame Pinnevinnette?
Yvonne Pinnevinnette!

Lucien, furious, advances on Joseph and drives him DS *like a big cat stalking its prey*

Lucien No, Monsieur, we are not the Pinnevinnettes!

Joseph, retreating DR *in front of Lucien and Yvonne, finds himself gradually cornered against the bedside table. Yvonne follows her husband in a pincer movement, which puts her at his right*

Yvonne Do we look like the Pinnevinnettes?

Lucien The Pinnevinnettes are on the other side of the landing.

Joseph (*in a choked voice*) But this is the right of the landing, isn't it?

Lucien No, Monsieur, it is the left! It's the right when you come out of the lift, but the left when you come up the stairs.

Yvonne If you had used the staircase like everyone else!

Joseph (*abruptly*) Oh, my God!

Yvonne
Lucien } (*together*) What is it?

Joseph But then . . . this means that I shall have to break the news all over again?

Lucien (*taking him by the arm and leading him* C) You don't imagine that I am going to do it for you?

Joseph Oh, but to have to start again! When I was so relieved to have got it over.

Lucien (*advancing on him again*) Was there ever such an imbecile?

Yvonne (*advancing on him from the other side*) To come here and upset us by saying that Mama was dead when she wasn't!

Joseph Madame, I am terribly sorry.

Yvonne (*shrugging her shoulders*) Oh, shut up! (*She moves away* DR)

Lucien (*turning him round and propelling him* US) Now, get out! Idiot!

Yvonne (DS, *below the bed*) Bungler!

Lucien (*returning* DL, *by the fireplace*) Fool!

Joseph (*at the back*) But, sir, it wasn't my fault! Besides, you ought to be happy!

Lucien
Yvonne } (*together*) Happy!

Lucien Brute!

Yvonne Lunatic!

Lucien Cretin!

Joseph (*in the doorway*) It's beyond me; you bawl me out because your mother's not dead! You ought to be pleased!

Lucien
Yvonne } (*together, converging on him*) { What do you mean? What are you talking about?

Lucien (*at the L of the door, to Joseph*) Will you get out! In the name of God!

Yvonne (*pushing Joseph out*) Just go!

Joseph (*as he is being pushed out*) I shan't forget this!

Yvonne Nor shall we!

Yvonne follows Joseph out and pursues him on to the landing

Lucien stays by the door and continues to hurl abuse at Joseph

Lucien Get out!
Yvonne (*off*) Oh!
Lucien Get out!
Yvonne (*off*) Oh!
Lucien Get out!
Yvonne (*off*) Oh!
Lucien Get out!
Yvonne (*off*) Oh!
Lucien Get out!
Yvonne (*off*) Oh!

Mixed with these exclamations are the protestations of the invisible Joseph, the sound of the front door being opened and then slammed shut behind him

Lucien returns DS and addresses a final growl to no-one in particular

Lucien Get out!

Yvonne returns

Yvonne (*overwrought, returning to the foot of the bed, throwing her head-scarf and cloak on it*) Oh!

Lucien Oh!

Yvonne Oh!

Lucien What a brute!

Yvonne To give us such a shock! (*She sits, exhausted, on the bench*)

Lucien (*indignantly*) Oh! (*After a moment, seizing the initiative*) She has a lot to answer for, *your* mother!

Yvonne What?

Lucien You see what she has done to us now, *your* mother!

Yvonne (*stunned*) What do you mean? What are you talking about?

Lucien What am I going to say to the decorator now? When he discovers that your mother isn't dead, after all? That the whole thing was a mistake?

Yvonne What do you mean, when he discovers? He knows nothing about it.

Lucien (*almost crying*) But I have written to him!

Yvonne (*standing up, indignantly*) Already!

Lucien Certainly! As he was making such a nuisance of himself!

Yvonne Oh!

Lucien I told him I would be able to settle up with him, having had the . . . the misfortune to lose my mother-in-law.

Yvonne That's too much! You were going to cash in on your expectations from Mama!

Lucien How could I know it was all a mistake! It's just like your mother to play a trick like that on us! (*He beats his fist on the hall door*) Oh, the cow! The cow!

Yvonne (*jumping on him like a tigress*) Who are you calling a cow? Is it Mama you're calling a cow?

Lucien (*abandoning all restraint*) Yes, yes, yes! Cow! Cow!

Yvonne (*trying to scratch his face with her nails*) Beast! Beast!

At this point there is a ringing, different and more distant than the front doorbell, which breaks up their quarrel

(*Sharply*) Oh, shut up!

Lucien (*taken by surprise*) Who's that?

Yvonne It must be Annette ringing at the side door.

Lucien (*moving* DS) I shall go mad!

Yvonne (*suddenly rejoicing*) Oh, Lucien, think! It's the neighbours who have lost their mother! It's the neighbours whose mother has died!

Lucien You're rejoicing in the misfortunes of others, are you?

Yvonne (DR, *sitting happily on the bed*) Why not! When I think it could have been us!

Lucien So it could! (*He moves* US) You're right, after all; look on the bright side. We're lucky.

Annette enters from the hall in a large, long overcoat belonging to Lucien

Annette There! It's dud!
Lucien (*rushing over to her and seizing her by the wrists*) The letters! What have you done with the letters?
Annette (*retreating into the space* US *of the bed*) I've pud theb id the post.
Lucien (*giving up*) That's it, then! She has put them in the post!
Annette Yes, as Bodsieur . . .
Lucien A fine mess you've made of things! Why did you have to be in such a hurry?
Annette But it was you that said to be, just a bobend ago . . .
Lucien Because a moment ago Madame's mother was dead. (*He returns* DS)
Yvonne (*radiantly, to Annette*) Yes, and now . . . she isn't!
Annette Oh, my God! They've all god bad!
Yvonne (*gladly*) It's not Mama! It's the neighbours' mother! The servant came to the wrong apartment.
Annette Dough! Is it true?
Lucien (*still furious about the letters*) Yes!
Annette (*jumping in the air with joy*) Oh, I ab so pleased, I'b so pleased!
Lucien (*still furious*) She's pleased, she's pleased!
Annette Yes, of course, aren't you?
Yvonne My husband is the only one who regrets it.
Lucien (*shrugging his shoulders*) Oh, well!
Yvonne He would have been happy to bury Mama.
Lucien Oh, well, "Bury"! (*Abruptly*) Oh, my God!
Yvonne (*alarmed*) What is it?
Lucien My letter to Borniol!
Yvonne What letter to Borniol?
Lucien (*rapidly, in a distressed voice*) I have written to Borniol, the undertaker, asking him to call at your mother's house tomorrow morning to make arrangements for the funeral!
Yvonne (*on her knees on the bed*) You've done what!
Lucien Oh, well! I was going to give her a splendid funeral!
Yvonne You want to kill her! You're wishing her dead!
Lucien Oh, no! It's not as bad as all that! We can cancel it by sending him a telegram tomorrow morning!

Yvonne (*shaking her fist at him*) Wretch! You want to kill Mama, you want to kill Mama!

All the following speeches overlap till the final curtain

Lucien (*going to the front of the bed, imperiously*) That's enough of that! It's time we went to sleep!
Yvonne (*without pausing*) Villain! Assassin! Murderer!
Lucien (*half-mounted on the bench*) Will you shut up? Be quiet!
Annette (*on the edge of the bed, trying to come between them*) Badarb! Bodsieur!
Yvonne He wants to kill Mama! He wants to kill Mama!
Lucien (*abandoning his place and turning to front*) I'm not putting up with this; I'd rather sleep in the maid's sheets!

The curtain begins to fall

Yvonne And he says I have breasts like a coat-hanger!
Annette Badarb, Badarb!
Lucien (*reaching the door* L) Damn it! Damn it!
Yvonne (*wailing*) He says I have breasts like a coat-hanger!
Lucien Damn it!

Lucien exits in a temper

CURTAIN

FURNITURE AND PROPERTY LIST

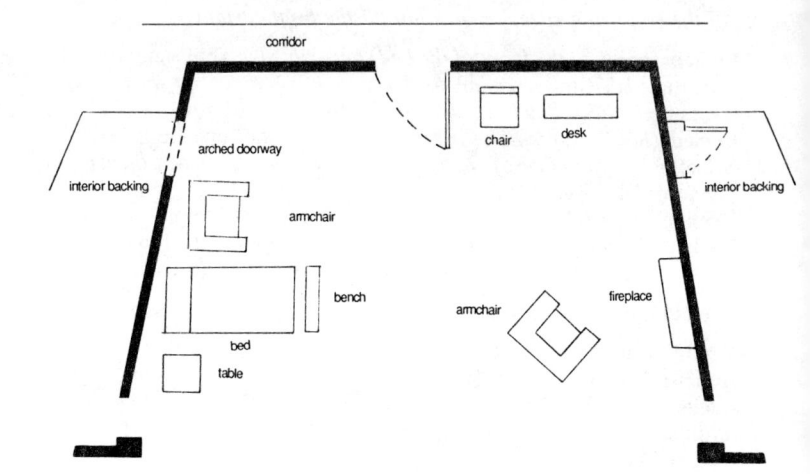

On stage: Bed and bedding. *On foot:* lady's robe
Bench
Armchair. *On it:* lady's petticoat, vest
Writing-desk. *In it:* writing materials, letter-cards
Chair
Bed-side table. *On it:* nightlight (lit), medicine bottle with cork
Small armchair
Fireplace. *Above it:* mirror *On mantelpiece:* candlesticks, clock, tray with carafe of water and glasses, tea-making apparatus, box of matches
On walls: modern prints, Japanese fans etc.
Yvonne's slippers on floor downstage of bed
Lucien's slippers upstage of bed

Off stage: Lighted candle, Cane and umbrella (**Lucien**)
Packet of camomile and sugar basin (**Annette**)
Salt-cellar (**Annette**)
Lucien's suit, shoes and hat (**Annette**)
Travelling clothes (**Yvonne**)

LIGHTING PLOT

Practical fittings required: electric chandelier
Interior. A bedroom.

To open: Room in darkness except for nightlight

Cue 1   **Lucien** switches on chandelier
            Snap on chandelier and full covering lighting   (Page 3)

EFFECTS PLOT

Cue 1	Five seconds after Curtain rises *Doorbell rings—repeated after ten seconds*	(Page 1)
Cue 2	**Yvonne:** "Who is it?" *Doorbell rings*	(Page 2)
Cue 3	**Yvonne** gets out of bed *Doorbell rings twice*	(Page 2)
Cue 4	**Yvonne:** (*off*) "I might have known!" *Sound of front door being unlocked*	(Page 2)
Cue 5	Yvonne: (*off*) "How inconsiderate of you." *Door shutting and relocking of front door*	(Page 2)
Cue 6	**Lucien:** "Oh, no! Hardly any . . ." *Clock strikes four*	(Page 3)
Cue 7	**Lucien:** "There's no need to kick me like that!" *Doorbell rings. Pause, then bell rings again*	(Page 18)
Cue 8	**Lucien:** "It must be the front door." *Doorbell rings*	(Page 18)
Cue 9	**Lucien:** "Yes." *Doorbell rings*	(page 19)
Cue 10	**Yvonne:** "You're a man, but as for me . . ." *Doorbell rings*	(Page 19)
Cue 11	**Yvonne:** "What? Oh! Yes!" *Doorbell rings repeatedly*	(Page 19)
Cue 12	**Annette:** (*off*) "Huh! Agaid!" *Doorbell rings*	(Page 19)

Night Errant   45

Cue 13	**Yvonne:** "You'll bring bad luck!" *Prolonged ringing on doorbell*	(Page 20)
Cue 14	**Annette:** "I'b dot doig eddy bore!" *Doorbell rings*	(Page 21)
Cue 15	**Lucien:** "Don't cry like that, my dear, don't cry!" *Sound of safety chain being taken off and* *front door opened, which is then closed* *and the safety chain is replaced*	(Page 21)
Cue 16	**Yvonne:** (*off*) "Oh!" (5th time) *Sound of front door being opened, then* *slammed shut*	(Page 38)
Cue 17	**Yvonne:** "Beast, beast!" *Side-door bell rings*	(Page 39)